WILLIAM SCHUMAN

AMERICAN FESTIVAL OVERTURE

FOR ORCHESTRA

All rights of performance and broadcast strictly reserved.
Orchestra parts may be obtained for rental from the publisher.

ED - 3779

G. SCHIRMER, Inc.

Distributed by
Hal Leonard Publishing Corporation
7777 West Bluemound Road P.O. Box 13819 Milwaukee, WI 53213

ISBN 0-7935-1358-8

LIST OF INSTRUMENTS

* Flutes
  3rd Flute (interchangeable with Piccolo)
*2 Oboes
  English Horn
*2 Clarinets in B♭
  Bass Clarinet in B♭
*2 Bassoons
  Contrabassoon (*ad libitum*)
*4 Horns in F
  3 Trumpets in C
  3 Trombones
  Tuba
  Timpani
  Xylophone ⎫
  Snare Drum ⎬ 3 Players
  Cymbals ⎪
  Bass Drum ⎭
  1st and 2nd Violins
  Violas
  Violoncellos
  Contrabasses

*The Woodwind pairs and the Horns may be doubled.

Duration: about 8½ m.

"American Festival Overture" was composed for the special concerts of American music given by the Boston Symphony Orchestra. It was first played by this orchestra under Serge Koussevitzky on October 6, 1939. For the program book of this concert the composer supplied an analysis of the work. Space permits us to quote only the first paragraph:

The first three notes of this piece will be recognized by some listeners as the "call to play" of boyhood days. In New York City it is yelled on the syllables "Wee-Awk-Eee" to get the gang together for a game or a festive occasion of some sort. This call very naturally suggested itself for a piece of music being composed for a very festive program music. In fact, the idea for the music came to mind before the origin of the theme was recalled. The development of this bit of "folk material", then, is along purely musical lines.

American Festival Overture

William Schuman

MENO MOSSO,
a tempo

leggier-
mente

80

leggier-
mente

80

85

90

95

100

39299

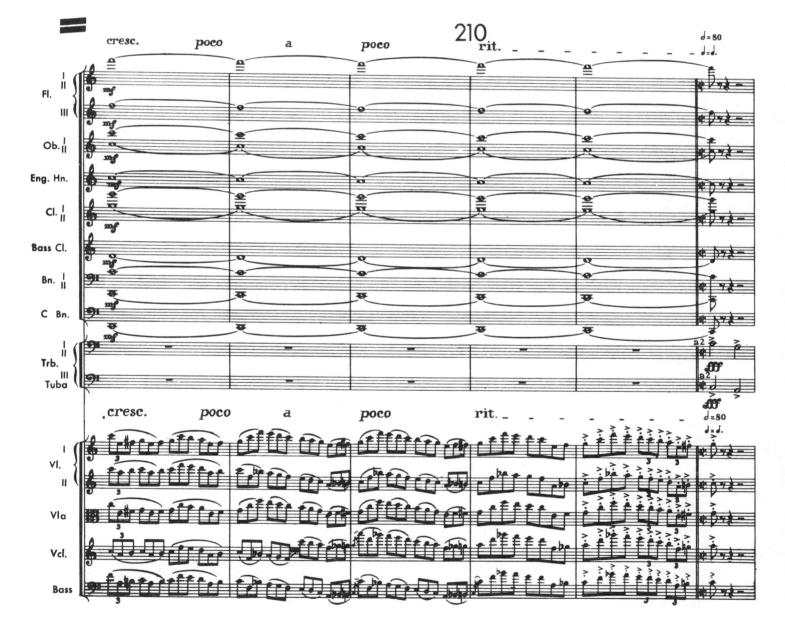

UN POCO
PRESTO

39299

295

295

315

330

330

335
Fl. I II
III
Ob. I II
Eng. Hn.
Cl. I II
Bass Cl.
Bn. I II
C Bn.
Hn. I II
III IV
Tpt. I
II
III
Trb. I II
III
Tuba
Timp.
Perc.
Vl. I
II
Vla
Vcl.
Bass
335

350